T0030599

THE UNBOXING OF A BLACK GIRL

THE UNBOXING OF A BLACK GIRL

OF A

BLACK GIRL

Angela Shanté

PAGE STREET YA

PAGE STREET YA

Copyright © 2024 Angela Shanté
First published in 2024 by
Page Street Publishing Co.
27 Congress Street, Suite 1511
Salem, MA 01970
www.pagestreetpublishing.com

Distributed by Macmillan, sales in Canada by The Canadian Manda Group.

28   27   26   25   24   1   2   3   4   5

ISBN-13: 979-8-89003-953-8
Library of Congress Control Number: 2023945463

Cover and book design by Emma Hardy for Page Street Publishing Co.
Cover art © Nancey B. Price

Printed and bound in the United States

for girls who are told to shrink into boxes
to tighten into spaces too small for you,

for The Culture,

but mostly

for Black girls/women.

FROM THE AUTHOR

It has taken me years to let go of this collection. Not because I
didn't have the words, or the structure. I knew exactly what this
would say, how it would breathe on the page. The pieces were
always there. But, I don't think *I* was ready. You see, to me, poetry
is the most vulnerable form of writing.

In the past, it has been my refuge in times of crisis. It was the
vehicle I used to tell my mother about my sexual assault years
after The Incident. And later in life, when I wanted to quit
teaching because I felt helpless to a broken system, I found my
way through it with spoken word. Poetry and experimental
storytelling have always anchored me when the rainbow truly
wasn't enough.[1]

The initial rendition of this collection took shape as part of my
MFA thesis at City College of New York. In the beginning, it was
a quippy critique about Black girlhood in America. But then 2020
happened, and *The Unboxing* shifted into something much, much
more.

I've been collecting these poems for years, both as a way to heal
forward and as a way of understanding my past. As a way to talk
to my younger self and chart the waters for what I am becoming.
It is truly the book I wish I had as a young adult.

Toni Morrison once said, "If there's a book that you want to read,
but it hasn't been written yet, then you must write it." So, I did.
And now I am giving it to you, in the hopes that you can use it in
your own unboxing . . . so, eventually, we can all be free.

----

1 For older readers: *for colored girls who have considered suicide / when the
rainbow is enuf* by Ntozake Shange

for
the elders[2]
the aunties
the sisters
>women who wore heavy names
>that sit on your tongue
>names carved by culture.
>these poems are for you,

for
the ones who got to grow up
and the ones who didn't

for the ones
forced to shoulder
adulthood
on flat chests

for the girls who are *still*
>—still developing
>—still growing
>—still learning and mistaking
>—still finding ways to be soft
in a world hard on Black girls

hard on Black babies
hard on Black bodies
hard on Black joy
hard on Black beauty
hard on Black birth
hard on Black children.

---

2 My elders: Shirley, Arlene, Catherine, Adell, Beatrice, Trini, Alice, Lynn, Fanny, Shawn, and Alice

and,
eternally,
for the unbridled women
who run with wolves[3]
and season their food with love

I write these poems for you,

Thank you,

— From Angela With Love

3 BOOK RECOMMENDATION: *Women Who Run With the Wolves: Myths and Stories of the Wild Woman Archetype* by Clarissa Pinkola Estés

CONTENTS

I

THE BOXES WE SEE

*Black girls learn duality early.
too early.*

conflicts inside. conflicts outside.

some boxes are chosen for us.

*being aware of boxes and
escaping them are two different
things.*

Black girls learn duality early.

too early.

ALLOW ME TO REINTRODUCE MYSELF[4]

I was a meek girl.
out of place
in my neighborhood.
       too soft
for the sharp edges
that outlined my world,

          and New York City will eat you whole.

But.
I grew
and learned
from the women
who,
       brown-faced, like mine
were
       going and coming
       leading and following
were
       healed and processing
       wounded and unlearning

how to be girls
and women
at the same time.

In a world hellbent on shoving them
       you
       us,
into a box.   *as if.*

---

4 This is a spoken word piece. It is meant to be read out loud. See how it feels on your tongue. Swallow it and repeat.

THE BOXES WE SEE

pre-date us
        boy,
        girl
binary thinking
for a binary world

ill-fitting boxes
        this,
        or that
manufactured boxes
designed
        to "protect"
        to control
        to shield
binary boxes
for a binary world

when we are young
these are the boxes that we see
and swallow

because children are to be seen
and not heard

so
we fold
and bend
shift and break
to fit into them,

boxes wrapped in religion
        in patriarchy
        in capitalism
        in hate

boxes that help us survive
a jagged-edged world

BOYS VS. GIRLS[5]

before I could walk
I knew there was a difference
between boys and girls.

---

5 This is a 5-7-5 haiku.

SINGLE-PARENT (NOUN)

/ˈsiŋ-gəl/ /ˈper-ənt/

:someone raising a child/ren without a partner

My mother was a "single-parent," by choice. Felt and lived by the ancient ancestral saying that she'd rather be *alone than unhappy*.[6] I always saw it as a strength. But that's not the way the world saw it.

Outside. The term single-parent wandered into my life in elementary school. An utterance by some school adult. A cluster of words that seemed odd to my young ears. Because, yes, my mother was a single parent, but the way the adult flung the words my way made it understood that *being* a single-parent should be avoided. At. All. Costs.

Like somehow my mother (void of a man/father/husband) was less than. Less than a woman? Something to be pitied?

But that's the thing about being inside and outside The Culture.

Inside. My mother, like many other Black mothers, sought community. My father's side of the family lived in Brooklyn. We saw Grandma Shirley, Auntie Hope, and Uncle Jermaine often, but Ma raised us uptown, in the Bronx, with her mother (Meemaw) and her side of the family. A blended family with deep roots in the South, made up of play cousins and blood strangers.

---

6 "It's Not Right, But It's Okay," written by LaShawn Daniels, Rodney Jerkins, Fred Jerkins III, Isaac Phillips, Toni Estes; recorded by the one and only Whitney Houston

THE TALK #1

my mother never minced words.
No cute nicknames
for private parts
or lying about why
Christmas missed us[7]

she wanted us to know
that we had community
a culture
a home
a safe space
to land.
In a hard
hard
world.

---

7 The Notorious B.I.G, born Christopher Wallace, said this lyric in the CLASSIC,
"Juicy."

BLACK GIRLS VS. THE WORLD

I want to live in a world
where Black girls get to hold on to their childhood.
Get to
sweet sixteen and quinceañera
their sweetheart crush
      right before curfew
      and the streetlights come on

I want to live in a world
where Black girls get to be safe
get to frolic in fields with their shoes off
and inspect insects
      inspect innocence
      with careless abandonment[8]

I want to live in a world where Black girls get to be free

---

8 I wish people would stop calling the cops on Black and Brown children simply
being . . . children.

INHERITED

we inherited these boxes
from elders who ripened too soon
like bruised strange fruit[9]
swaying from poplar trees

but

we inherited these gifts
these hands
these words
these curves
from elders who ripened too soon
like bruised strange fruit
swaying from poplar trees

and

we inherited this moment
this style
this movement
this freedom
from elders who ripened too soon
like bruised strange fruit
swaying from poplar trees

---

9 "Strange Fruit," written by Abel Meeropol; recorded by Nina Simone. No notes; just go listen.

THE ELDERS

were once girls
who dreamt wildly,
who loved softly.

They were once girls
who wanted to be gentle
who sought comfort

but their childhoods were ushered out the door
like unwanted house guests

for survival
for protection
in preparation.

We looked to them
both
to show us how to wear our womanhood
and
how not to.

THE TALK #19

Meemaw:
       measured skirts with rulers
       insisting on modesty
       in her house
       and presence
       because girls are
       to be seen
       and not heard

SALT-N-PEPA[10]

My sister and I were born
eighteen months apart
A February Aquarius
and an August Leo

growing up
people often said we could pass
as twins
but

my fair skin
        shades lighter than
        her brown hues
meant the world would
        get-out-that-sun, her
        and
        she's-so-pretty, me

a paper bag[11] thin
distinction
like a thousand tiny cuts
we never asked for.

---

10 Salt-N-Pepa is an African American Hip Hop group made up of three
women. Their lyrics are political and empowering.
11 RESEARCH: The Brown Paper Bag Test

conflicts inside. conflicts outside.

FIRST-CHILD SYNDROME

I don't remember my sister
ever
being little

like a *baby*
baby

i don't remember her
ever being small

like a girl
young
innocent

she's always been
a sister-mother
to me

her childhood,
snapshots
remembered in flickers
mini moments
strung together
by Polaroids.

SISTER-MOTHER

my sister
her brown hands
      too small for braiding
pony-tailed my hair every morning,
beat bullies off me every afternoon,
and cooked dinner every night

she perfected signatures on parent-forms
and walked me to school every morning
and picked me up from the community
      center in the afternoon
she was the eldest.
by eighteen months

so her brown hands
      too small for braiding
shielded me
and took the brunt of it all.

THE TALK #53[12]

eat or be eaten
sink, swim, or learn how to tread.
just try to survive.

---

12 This is a 5-7-5 haiku.

FLOSS (VERB)

/fläs/

:to flaunt

Learning that we were poor was the first of many hard life lessons. It was a pill, initially, too bitter to swallow; a realization that I was not yet ready (nor willing) to accept freely. I mean, sure, at a young age I knew the phrases *make a penny stretch* and *shop on sale*. But that didn't make us poor. *Right?*

By eight years old, Ma had taught my siblings and I to count (and match up) our change with the receipt *before* leaving the store. And we definitely never skipped this step because, as she liked to say, *money doesn't grow on trees*. Aren't these lessons that *all* kids learn though?

In my prepubescent brain we were not poor because we always had money, never lived on the streets, didn't have holes in our clothes, and we got an allowance. For an inner-city girl these were luxuries of a Material Girl. Poor people don't have luxuries. *Right?*

Having luxuries placed you in a tier above. I knew that if I had something I could flaunt over another person, the world would treat me a little nicer. Hold me a little gentler. So, allowance was a big get. It meant my big sister and I were a pair of the very few girls in our hood who had money to spend. Having extra was a big floss.

It meant freedom. It meant we were the envy of our friends and at the top of the social totem pole (even if it was short-lived). It meant penny candies and quarter-water juices after school. It meant bribes and favors. It meant subway rides to the Bronx Zoo on Wednesdays and Coney Island tokens on the weekend. And once in a while, when we resisted the urge of the initial splurge and actually *saved* some of it, it meant buying something to floss. And people who had something to floss definitely were *not* poor.

FOOD DESERT[13]

I didn't know this then,
always thought the
Sunday bus ride
to other neighborhoods
outer boroughs
was my mother's attempt to
bond.

---

13 Look around your neighborhood at the resources available to you and your
family. What do you notice? What do you wonder?

THEN AND NOW

she inherited,
some boxes from her mother . . .
wash, rinse, and repeat.

ON TIKTOK I WATCHED

a mother cut off
her daughter's hair because she
"needed discipline"

THE TALK #11

there are some people who
you can't save.
some don't want saving.
and others
who only want to be
the savior.

some boxes are chosen for us.

THREE THE HARD WAY

My mother's house was soft:
    gentle.
    shoes off at the door.
    we were allowed to be little girls
    there.
    were allowed to explore
    to question
    to laugh
    and love
    hard.

Meemaw's house
was always put together
    plastic on couches
orderly.
    like everything had a place
and it betta' be
        in
    that
place.

Brooklyn was
a warm Caribbean blend
of roti and hugs
dominos and spades
extended family
and
queer
love.

CODE-SWITCHING (NOUN)

/kōd - ˈswɪchɪŋ/

:the practice of/the ability to alternate between two or more
languages

I learned how to code-switch by watching the women in my
family. The Elders. The Matriarchs. Women who *knew a thing
or two*. Women who taught me how to be tough and soft. How to
stare someone down and hold space for sorrow. Women who had
survived.

Outside. I marveled at my grandmother's range to softness when
conducting business with *important* people. An eye that could
pierce metal. Stiff shoulders in the front pew of church. Shirts
starched. Pants pleated. Orderly.

Inside. There is a more subtle switch we adorn: a relaxed, familial
mask that we sometimes slip on and out of effortlessly. Boxes
within boxes.

I learned that even at home we needed to make adjustments. My
mother's usually relaxed smile stiffened when we arrived at her
mother's house. In Brooklyn, Grandma Shirley and her children
learned to tiptoe around their queerness. A soft-spoken need to
keep the peace and respect elders. A shrinking box of sorts.

A deposition for one person. A shift in attitude for another. A
twirling tightrope of exhaustion.

Is this why Black women are always so tired?[14]

---

14 BOOK RECOMMENDATION: *Rest Is Resistance: A Manifesto* by Tricia
Hersey

IN THE MIDDLE

for a long time it was just my mother,
my sister and I.
I was the baby.

then Ma got pregnant.
I think my sister and I
wanted another sister.
but it was
         a boy.

THE TALK #17

growing up our apartment was a turnstile
for every cousin and play cousin within
the greater 'up north' region.
we always had someone sleeping on the couch,
        or floor.
a distant cousin coming from the South.
a foster kid from down the block.

that is to say,

my mother welcomed almost everyone into our space.
and if she did so
you were family.
full stop.

and no matter what is happening inside,
family sticks together outside.

TOXIC (ADJECTIVE/NOUN)
/ˈtäk-sik/
:related to something harmful and/or dangerous; harmful and/or
dangerous behavior that adds negativity to your life

We didn't have the word *toxic* growing up. In fact, up until
my mother's generation our family (like many Black families)
hardly talked about mental health inside, let alone outside, of our
community (and with great reason).[15]

Inside. When Ma started to go to therapy, Meemaw sucked her
teeth and we never spoke of it again. In Meemaw's generation
they didn't talk about such things. They didn't like to speak about
the things they didn't have names for . . . and unpacking trauma
takes time. Meemaw's generation didn't have the time.

But more to the heart of things, peeling back the layers is hard.
Being honest about feelings and needs is hard. It's easier to sweep
things under the rug. Tuck things away. But that's the thing about
things that go untreated and unsaid . . . sometimes they fester
over. They become cancerous.

Outside. I learned that simply being a girl meant I was expected
to just deal with toxicity. Be seen, not heard. Be still. Be feminine.
Smile. And, being a Black girl meant I was also expected to
simultaneously be strong in the face of it all. Toxic customs. Toxic
systems. Toxic ideologies. Toxic culture. And toxic boys/men.

---

15 America has a long history of medical racism.

UNCLES

were once boys
who were forced to shoulder
manhood
on narrow chests

boys who are *still*
   —still developing
   —still growing
   —still learning and mistaking
and finding ways to be soft
in a world
hard on Black babies
hard on Black bodies
hard on Black beauty
hard on Black birth
hard on Black boys.

FAST[16] (ADVERB/ADJECTIVE)

/fast/

:a derogatory way to describe a *girl* who steps outside of
respectability boxes

My mom lived by her favorite motto: *education is the key* (and
therapy had made her very introspective). Because of this, she
never stopped trying to expand our world. My siblings and I were
put into every free after school program in the neighborhood.
Dance classes (tap, jazz, African, modern), sport teams (swim and
basketball were my favorite). If we could walk there, we were
going.

Ma also wanted us to be prepared for the world that we were
growing up in. So naturally, this included giving us all of The
Talks. By nine years old, I had already had several Talks with her.

When a white elementary school teacher had been bewildered
by my intelligence, we had The Talk about racism and implicit
bias. After they installed police officers on every corner of our
neighborhood, we had The Talk about the history of policing
in America. And, because my mother was a sex-positive parent,
we'd also had several of The Talks about girls, boys, gender, and
sexuality.

Outside. I learned all the ways to avoid being classified as fast. I
learned that *I* (a young girl) shouldn't tempt boys and/or men. All
of the Don'ts. All of the Shouldn'ts. All of the Can'ts. All of the
ways I should dress. And not dress. All of the ways I should speak.
And not speak. All of the ways I should carry myself. And not
carry myself. I learned how I should respond to and interact with
boys/men. And how not to.

(continued)

---

16 One of the first sexual boxes young girls are placed in. RESEARCH: the
adultification of Black girls.

I welcomed these lessons and parameters. After all, I saw how the world treated girls/women who stepped out of these boxes . . . and I honestly didn't want any of that smoke.[17]

---

17 My brother, on the other hand, did not have this worry.

PRECIOUS[18]

Black girlhood is made
of fragile rice paper, and
can be gone like that.

---

18 A 5-7-5 haiku dedicated to Sapphire, the author of *Push*

BUCKWILD (VERB)

/bək-ˈwīld/

:acting insane or out of control; unable to be controlled

Ma used to call our house The Naked House. When we got home, my sister and I always stripped down to our undergarments in the living room. My sister called it the Hippie House. I didn't really have a name for it, I just knew it was home. I knew it was safe.

Our apartment was on the second floor of a prewar building in the Bronx. Ma let Sharise and I take the bigger bedroom in the back because she said "little girls need light to grow." But even with all the light, my favorite room was the living room.

The living room was for gathering, and communion. It was where Ma taught us about agency and sexuality. Where she taught us about womanhood and menstruation. Where she showed us how to use condoms and avoid STDs.[19]

It was also where she argued with Meemaw about us being buckwild girls in need of taming.

---

19 My mother taught the sex-education class at the community center in our neighborhood.

THEY SAY[20]

they say we are strong
because we are Black.
and we can feed a hungry soul
or fill a desolate child's belly with love
and we don't break, bend, or crack under pressure
we toughen.

they say we are beautiful
because we are Black.
and our skin reflects pigments of Africa
our smile stretches across the lagoons of the South
to the steel and concrete of the North.

they say we are brave
because we are Black.
and our eyes have seen through generations
there's beauty in surviving.
but there's peace in thriving

they say,
and I agree

---

20 This is a spoken word piece. Read it out loud. See how it feels on your tongue.
Swallow it and repeat.

STRONG BLACK WOMAN TROPE

we grow.
through despair,
like roses
from concrete.
we numb.
propaganda sirens,
piercing our
dreams.
we toughen.
through
single homes
baby-self-sitting
dinner-making.
we want tough skin.
to make it.
day after day.

we stand.
on picket lines,
with mourning mothers
overlooking the small spaces
we are forced to fit in.
our place in the
American opportunity
our addendum to *his*-story
rape culture, and
the patriarchy.
when really, *shit*.
we are simply trying to make it
day after day.

But what y'all hear is
Black women can fix it.

Black women will do the work.
Black women are strong.
Black women are superhuman.

because illusions are palatable . . .

in reality
we crumble,
waver, like
   bulbs in old street lamps
we break
   underneath it all
we wither
after being
   worn, rinsed
     and reused
like hand-me-down jeans.
we fall,
too . . .
like towers once up high
  from hate
  from ignorance
  from expectations
  from adultification
there's oppression in our education.
oppression in our water.
in our air.
in our textbooks.
  he came
  he saw
  he conquered
  she sewed the flag
we are constantly reteaching.
unlearning.
but, after the S-branded red cape
  has been discarded
    the all-day

work shoes are
　　　　in their proper place
kids fed
　　　　properly bathed
　　　　　　　　homework
checked
　　　　bills paid
dishes done
　　　　floor swept
　　　　　　　　locks secure
　　　　lights out.
She will lay down, briefly
before preparing
for the next day

being aware of boxes and escaping them are two different things.

THE TALK #2

Meemaw was a saved woman
believed that religion
would set us free
held Bible verses on her tongue
at the quick
        hymns over hugs
        scripture over softness
because if you spare the rod
you'll spoil the child

DIVORCE (NOUN/VERB)
/di-ˈvȯrs/
:a splitting of two parties

Black folks have a way of watering down words we deem *too* harsh for our mouths. And so, instead of discussing my parent's divorce, the adults used words like *split*, *separate*, and *apart*; synonyms used to tiptoe around reality. Smaller. Quieter words are more palatable to swallow.

My parents met in high school. My mother. A young bride of eighteen. My father. Like many other Black men, enlisted in the army before his Adam's apple had grown. Both searching for their form of freedom. Looking for liberation. A life away from America.

And in a blink of an eye, they had two children under two years old, and my mother was boarding a bus back to New York City with us in tow.

In the Bronx we lived with my Meemaw for months. My mother would learn to smile without her teeth. She'd teach us to water down our temper. We learned to curb, adjust, bend, and retreat. We learned to go to school and come straight home to do our homework. Keep our heads down. Eat. Wash. Repeat.

QUEER

My aunt and uncle
tiptoed
around Shirley
for years
understood that it was
her
house.
so
they learned to curb,
anchored rainbow flags
And learned to
float around one another
slow inflating balloons
ready to pop

THE TALK #5

When my brother came to live with us
we learned that the world would treat him differently
that they would see his big brown eyes
and wide smile
and think
danger.
when all
I ever see
is my little
baby brother.

I SEE YOU BLACK BOY

and, I pray for you
that you continue to grow
and love and learn and laugh
and, simply
be.

I pray the world is kind to you
that it sees the brother I see
the one who loves
and learns
and laughs
without restrictions.

I pray that the universe protects you
that it covers you and guides your steps
toward love
and learning
and laughter,
without callousness.

in a world hell bent on not seeing you,
I see you Black boy.

GENERATIONAL HEALING (NOUN/ADJECTIVE)

/jen-ə-'rā-ʃən-əl/ /hēling/

:the healing of toxic traits, habits, customs, and beliefs inherited
from previous generations

My mother was the first to start The Healing in our immediate
family. She was raised by parents who didn't graduate high school
and she hooked onto the notion at an early age that education was
her key. Her key to options. Her way out.

When she was six, she was sent to live with her father in the
South where she would attend a newly desegregated school.[21]
Despite being spat on in the cafeteria, her time in the South
fueled her thirst for education. She saw how far her own father
had gotten with just a trade and street smarts, but wondered
where she could go with a high school diploma. So, despite the
options presented to her at the time (get a job or get married), she
decided to do what the generation before her had not. Complete
high school.

It was this small step that started her on her own different path.
One that diverged from Meemaw's, and her mother's. A path of
her own choosing.

---

21 If you know anything about the desegregation of schools in the 1970s, then
you know the time was pretty traumatic (especially for a Black kindergartener).

INTERGENERATIONAL HEALING[22]

starts off rather small,
tiny, like an avalanche

to a mustard seed.

---

22 This is a 5-7-5 haiku.

II

THE ONES WE DON'T

When do Black girls lose their childhood?

THE BOXES WE DON'T

are double-edged swords
that come
force-fed.
dripped in patriarchal blues[23]

are ribbon-wrapped
and lined with smallpox
blankets to keep us warm[24]

are the in-between spaces
sunken places[25]
deep,
  deep
    down
in the fabric of our nation

23 MUST READ: *Patriarchy Blues* by Frederick Joseph
24 MUST LISTEN: "American Terrorist" by Lupe Fiasco
25 MUST WATCH: *Get Out* by Jordan Peele

UNTITLED

i lost my childhood
on the way home from the Boys & Girls club
to an after-school counselor.

cracked shells littered the walk home
from the bodega
leaving evidence
of
my
innocence
behind
me.

TO MY INNOCENCE

childhood,
I wished I could pick you up
carry you with me,
a little longer
for
our journey wasn't complete
but the universe
had other plans

1995

Naively,
in the back of her mind
(although she'd never admit it)
she always assumed monsters never existed,
were some cockamamie story
adults tell children
to keep them in line
        like: helmets on bikes,
        or: look both ways before crossing a street
        (even on a one-way)
        and: always wear shorts under your skirt

naively,
in the back of her mind
(although she'd never admit it)
she believed monsters were
one-eyed
green-skinned
six-legged beings,
that spooked their way into the lives of
unsuspecting naughty children

naively,
in the back of her mind
(although she'd never admit it)
she didn't think there was anything wrong with
holding his hand,
sitting on his lap,
or going to the store to get sweets afterwards,
besides, he didn't have one eye
and she always wore her shorts underneath her skirt[26]

---

26 Most sexual assault (SA) cases are committed by relatives and family
friends. If you, or anyone you know has been a victim of SA there are
resources to support you at rainn.org.

BODEGA (NOUN)
/bō·dā·gə/
:the corner store in the hood

The summer I entered middle school, I was molested at the Boys & Girls Club. Not because of anything I did. I'd followed all of the rules. I crossed my legs. I wore shorts under my skirts. Up until this day, I'd strategically stood in the back. Didn't want to draw too much attention. And definitely wanted to float under the bully-radar.

Inside. I lost myself in books. In fictional places, little girls were allowed to be. Places where boogeymen and boxes don't exist. Aside from books, the Bodega was my second favorite place. Not because of the snacks, or because Julio gave out free pops in the summer, but because it was a neutral zone for all. A place where bullies couldn't bully. And sketchy people couldn't sketch.

After The Incident I hid in the Bodega because I knew He wouldn't follow me in. I had time to think.

Question.

Process.

Replay.

What happened to me. How it had happened to me. *Why* it had happened. Why it had happened to *me*. What I had done to *make* it happen to me. What had I *not* done to make this happen.

Outside. I fixed my clothes and walked up and down the aisle over and over, ignoring Julio's concerned eyes over the counter.

NOT-NOT-RAPE[27]

it was decided
for me, not by me (mind you)
that it was not rape

---

27 Sexual assault comes in many forms, if you believe you or someone you know
has been a victim of SA, contact the National Sexual Assault Hotline at 1-800-
656-4673.

AFTER IT[28]

I learned that
I wasn't unique.
I heard stories of friends
and friends-of-friends
girls who *got it worse*
ladies who *didn't get away*
and
other girls
and women
who live daily
with broken boys and
calloused men

---

28 Every seventy seconds someone is sexually assaulted. If you, or someone you
know, is in need of resources and support, find it at rainn.org.

SHIRLEY

I spent a lot of time
In Brooklyn
with my grandmother,
Shirley.
after The Incident.

she was a quiet lady
an albino Black woman
who wore her glasses at the tip of her nose
smoked Virginia Slims
and
lived in a building
located
on a
tree-filled street in Brooklyn.

not like the wispy trees
they planted on my block
in the Bronx
no.

a block straight out of
The Cosby Show[29]

---

29 We can feel nostalgic as a culture and hold people accountable. Both things
can happen at the same time.

I WAS A WOMAN?

now,
I think.

or at least
a young woman

but definitely

definitely

different.

GROWN (VERB/ADJECTIVE)

/grōn/

:referring to growing up and reaching maturity and acting as such

I decided not to tell my mother about The Incident. Not because I thought I was grown. But because I was ashamed.

I think.

So, I boxed it up and shouldered the blame in isolation. I replayed it in my head over and over trying to find the exact place where I went left when I should have gone right. Where did my yellow brick road veer up when it should have gone down? I avoided the community center until I graduated entirely and escaped to Brooklyn on the weekends.

This meant we needed to learn how to take the train. This meant my sister and I had to learn how to travel uptown and downtown. We learned what trains connected where. And of course, Meemaw and Ma had to give us all of The Talks associated with being two Black girls. Two Black girls who, up until this point, had never left our neighborhood unaccompanied.

Inside. I was terrified. But I was grateful at this moment to have a big sister.[30]

For a few weeks the adults shuttled us back and forth, sometimes riding with us both ways. But after a while we got a hang of the trip and were allowed to take the journey by ourselves. On a number train somewhere between the two boroughs my world grew.

---

30 A big sister who never let me forget that for the hour and a half it took us to step off the train in Brooklyn that she was in charge and I, being the *little* sister, needed to listen to her.

THE TALK #13

when navigating
outside our community

we were taught:
        to keep our heads on a swivel
        and keep an eye on one another.

        how to interact with cops
        and how not to.

        how to secure our backpacks
        and keep track of where we were.

and

if help *was* needed
we could find
safety
in Black women.

PERM (NOUN/VERB)

/pərm/

:a hairstyle produced by treating hair with chemicals so that it is relaxed

My mother didn't have many rules, but she did ask that we wait until we were teenagers before permanently altering anything on our bodies. No piercings. No tattoos. No perms. But every year, without fault, I pleaded with her to expedite her wait-until-you-are-a-teenager rule (which never worked).

Growing up, everyone in the hood wanted straight hair. This meant getting a perm. It didn't matter if it destroyed your curl pattern (which you were most likely to do), fried your edges (which was most likely to happen), or crisped your scalp (which would most likely take months to heal). Regardless of the strife it would cause, permed straight hair would instantly catapult you up the hood social chain.[31]

And here I was, entering middle school, the *only* one of my friends who still sported tightly coiled hair and thick braided plaits. I'd garnered the nickname of *Celie* from *The Color Purple* and . . . well, let's just say, I was trying to shake that name fast.

It's not that I hated my hair, but I didn't want to be outside of the cool-kid box. Plus, a perm would mean one less thing to worry about. One less problem to have to tackle. One less reason for someone to notice me. See me. Really *see* me.

And then . . . the day finally came . . . my Black Cinderella moment. My glow up. I dreamed about bouncing into school on Monday with tips swaying back and forth.

My mom was less ceremonial.

---

31 I didn't know it then, but this is a very anti-Black belief.

"Sit." (I sat)

"And don't move." (I wouldn't dream of it)

I closed my eyes to say goodbye to the old me. I wanted to solidify this moment in my head. Wanted to be able to journal my step into adolescence.

Grease. Part. Section. Lay flat. Hold.

And then the burn started . . .

It was a slow burn at first. A rising tingle grew from the base of my neck. My mother's legs tightening around me warned me not to move. Not to disrupt the ritual. To be in the moment. *Relax. Breathe.* So I did. I sat there, pressed between my mother's legs. Pressed between childhood and womanhood.

And I took it.

Where is her safe space?

ANXIETY (NOUN)
/aŋ-zī-ə-tē/
:a feeling of fear, dread, and uneasiness

After The Incident I suffered from anxiety. I found ways to cope and mask in school and at home. I learned to compartmentalize and find ways to forget it. Forget Him.

Outside. I found solace and comfort in numbers and storytelling. I liked discovering solutions and hidden patterns in math. And whenever I wasn't at school, my head was always in a book/ journal. On weekends an overstuffed backpack was carried from the Bronx to Brooklyn and back again.

Inside. I dealt with my emotions on the page. I wrote and read. It felt freeing to get it out and to get lost in someone's else's world.

And so I did so. A lot.

I told the page what I could not tell my mother. Words that I swallowed and turned into lyric.

THREE AND A POSS[32]

I learned how to play spades
over curry chicken
and shit talking
in a brownstone in Brooklyn

learned to lean in when I wanted to bluff
and spot a renege from three books away

a rite of passage
a moment in history
Black as spades

---

32 MUST DO: Learn how to play spades. "Three and a poss" = three books and
a possible fourth.

I WAS OBSESSED WITH QUINCY JONES GROWING UP

my Mother,
on her own journey
     of healing
brought home *Ebony* and *Essence* magazines
from her sales job
in Manhattan.

Our television:
     Black tv shows
     Black music
     Black films

a wide range of Blackness painted far and wide.

and then I found *The Wiz*.

THE WIZ[33]

has,
and always will be
one of my
top ten
Black masterpieces

when they peeked
behind the curtain
and found out
the Wiz
was Richard Pryor

and not

some
all-knowing
wish-granting
brains-making
heart-giving
courage-boosting
Wiz
that could save them.

chile'

I think about this message
a lot

---

33 MUST WATCH: *The Wiz*. Go watch it.

YOU CAN'T WIN

You're not a failure, you're just a product of negative thinking.
—Dorothy, *The Wiz*

The blaze of the sun has goldened your layers,
created a band of sweat underneath your makeshift hat

and it's only 9 a.m.

when you hear the drunken cries of The Crows
a wave of *shits* pass your usually restrained lips.
you think: *not today. Man, not today!*
but say: *hey fellas*

you strike your usual poise,
not wanting to ignite or upset the balance

it's only 10 a.m.

you think: *I wish I could nail them up here,*
but instead make an attempt at pleasantries
you attempt to impress with an educated quote you somehow
wrangled from between a piece of already-chewed gum and used
tissue

as the words crawl out of your throat
you wish you could swallow them back.
        Shit, shit, shit
they say: *you think you smart?*
punctuate that insult with: *you ain't smart*

I can't win

you know what comes next.
so you go numb
numb to the madness
numb to the heat

It's 11 a.m.

you've tuned it out, cast your eyes upward
but then
there is an unsettling silence.

Dorothy.
she flaps her scrawny arms
Shoo you jive turkeys,

and then come the words you've been waiting
for all your life:
I'll get you down,

And you think — *I can win*

THE TIN MAN[34]

is seeking a heart
something that might make him whole.
it comes from within.

34 This is a 5-7-5 haiku.

MEAN OLE LION

the cowardly lion
sits
upon his throne
overlooking the land
        the king.
able to get anything he wants
        at his beck and call
        outside.
but what he wants more than
anything
is to have courage
inside.

DOROTHY

was afraid to leave her neighborhood
she was happy being small
     there's safety in
     small.
     security
     in smallness.
     comfort.

but the thing about comfort
is
growth happens right   outside of it.

Where can she be free?

GIRLS AND WOMEN FOR OIL

she welcomes him with open arms
like a mother
like a daughter
though she is only thirteen
only beginning to understand.

she is a woman and he is a man
they teach her this
from every corner of the planet

when she ripens, the indentations on her thighs
will be the blueprints for missionaries to come
and
despite the disparity
when the Red Cross leaves
and the well-wishes and prayers
dry up
like all women,
she will continue to hope
            naïve and forgiving
she will welcome him
again and again
for Pepsi and bubble gum

this is how it should be
she is a woman and he is a man
she will birth a nation of bastard children
and continue to smile
she will become *The Breast Giver*[35]
and her childhood
gone
like a thief in the night

....

35 Go read it.

AFTER THE INCIDENT

it was hard to trust
anyone
anything
everyone
everything

but eventually
one day
became two
became a week
became a month
became a year . . .

FRESH AIR FUND (PROPER NOUN)

/freʃ er fənd/

:a not-for-profit organization that provided hood sabbaticals for
kids in NYC

In the 90s, they shipped Black and Brown kids out of inner-city
neighborhoods to be in nature. There were studies that showed
Black and Brown kids were adversely affected by systematic
racism in under-resourced neighborhoods in inner cities or
something like that (go figure). Either way, some well-meaning
white people got together with some well-meaning white people
with money and funded hood sabbaticals[36] for inner-city Black and
Brown children. These are their stories.[37]

I boarded a charter bus and left New York City for the first time
in 1993. I'd stacked my bookbag with books and snacks and used it
as a seat holder for my friend. We watched tall buildings fade into
green fields. Buses filled with Black and Brown children from all
five boroughs. We slept on cots in cabins and I, like many of the
kids, took to nature immediately. Archery was a particular favorite
of mine. I wrote home and told my mother about the overnight
in the woods, and the scary stories the girls liked to tell during
the night. I included a small lanyard necklace that I'd made in art
class with a kiss. I wanted her to know that I was having fun, and
I hoped she wasn't missing me too much.

---

36 If money allots, I recommend everyone take a hood sabbatical at least once a
year.
37 Just jokes.

Another Angela on a different side of the Bronx, would, like me, board a school bus to spend the summer living with a white family in upstate New York. She'd get her own comfy room or share a bunk with one of the biological siblings of the family who (for some reason) disdained her.[38] She'd take to swimming right away but would soon realize that being the only Black girl in an all-white space would mean her body was always up for consumption, and there are very few places to hide at a pool. Her hair would be touched repeatedly without consent or repercussions. She'd write home about wanting to come home, immediately. Instead of enjoying the fresh air and nature this hood sabbatical was supposed to provide, she would be paraded around all summer. A token.

---

38 Anti-Blackness usually starts at home.

THE TALK #7

when, I finally had a crush
I went to Ma and my sister
about it

I learned that
despite what people said
if someone has a crush on you
they should NOT treat you badly

CULTURE SHOCK

before summer camp
my world was pretty
Black
and
Brown

at sleepaway camp
a lot of our
counselors
came from
places I could
barely point to
on a map[39]

places with their own
languages
food
histories
struggles
places with their own boxes

---

39 Effects of under-resourced schools in the inner-city

SUMMER CAMP

days before autumn
could brown summer memories
we stood inside cool places
            where the sun couldn't touch us,
trees
woods
cabins
lazy days
and acoustic songs

days before autumn
could strip lush trees
we shared kisses in the dark,
sweaty hands,
your breath,
on my neck.
balancing being a teenager
on hard tiny cots

i remember you, Summer
red-violet sun rays
and
dark silent nights

sweet candy stars,
and saltwater tears,
untouched in a rural dreamland

and then,
after six weeks,
six weeks of Summer,
six weeks of you
we returned to the Bronx.
and I was
different.

THE SOUTH BRONX[40]

between the grime and litter
over burned buildings
and through smoke-filled highways
i can make out beauty

in the barrio of the Bronx
where Boriqua and Negro meant we all got along
spoke Spanglish
and spiced our food with Adobo

my best friend was Karen
and we spoke bongegeta all day long
listened to Hip Hop and one-two-three, kick'd
our ways to the store

where we purchased guava-flavored Now-and-Laters
sweet platanos from the Chinese restaurant
and played double dutch
or
watched stick ball
                              (until the street lights came on)
these blocks became our playgrounds
mattresses our leaping pad to dreams
tires our hiding places for hope
and alleys our adventure cueva

                                        (continued)

---

40 Spoken word piece previously published in *Promethean* Literary Magazine

aqui, we are home
hugged by graffiti-splattered walls
fast moving subways
Nuyoricans[41] are born
here

in the barrio of the Bronx
there was always amor
and despite your accent or shade
we were familia

---

41 If you are ever in NYC, you should check this place out.

MY SISTER RAN AWAY[42]

in a quest for her
own journey, own life, own dreams
and then there were two.

---

42 A haiku dedicated to my big sister.

Where does she get to just be?

PERIOD (NOUN/ADJECTIVE)
/ˈpirēəd/
:referring to the menstruation cycle

My mother and I have a great relationship now, but it wasn't always like this growing up. The day I got my period was one of those days. I remember the day vividly because my mother and I were having yet another heated debate. I don't remember exactly what the argument was about. But I do remember feeling like I was never, ever, going to forgive her. I stormed off to the bathroom. I wanted to be alone.

But seeing blood in my panties quickly broke that resolve.

In the bathroom, Ma's voice was warm and soothing. I sat on the edge of the toilet while she delivered the now-you-are-a-woman Talk. She explained this new phase of my life and I listened. I listened as she showed me how to balance the cotton submarine inside my underwear. Watched as she showed me how to take off the sanitary napkin. Practiced wrapping the discarded pad once . . . twice . . . three times.

After, we watched *The Wiz*, and she let me lay in her bed with the heating pad on my belly.

NOW I WAS A WOMAN?

after I started menstruating
I didn't want to go to school
didn't want to spend 5–7 days

stressing

worrying

looking

down

then

up

then

down

again.

didn't want to spend 5–7 days
raising my hand
and explaining why I had to
go to the bathroom

yes, again.

HIGH SCHOOL

My mother
and most mothers
on our block

knew the zoned schools were trash
not out of trying
but because of
        lack of funding
        and resources,
a perpetual broken system
        designed to miseducate
        under-educate
        subjected
Black history
Black culture
Black contributions
in
replace
of
American mythology.

these mothers
optioned for
charter
alternative
choice
spaces
to cut the pipeline[43]

they sent us away
        unclipped wings

to neighborhoods
beyond our borders

---

43 RESEARCH: The school-to-prison pipeline

THE TALK #3

Outside.
folks see Blackness
as this
or that

when in actuality
there isn't
one way
to
be
Black.

BLACK IS NOT A MONOLITH[44]

Dedicated to everyone who capitalizes the B in Black

it can not be boxed
it can not be defined, and
it can not be bought

Black is divine, see
Black can be anything we
decide it to be

---

44 Our Blackness cannot be placed in a box. A pair of 5-7-5 haikus

FOR BLACK GIRLS II[45]

take a beat, and rest.
enjoy the slow pace of life
don't rush to grow up.

---

45 This is a 5-7-5 haiku.

boxes inside, boxes outside

THE MAN IN THE MIRROR

when people talked about poverty
growing up
they would say
people are starving in Africa

but I knew,
that
people were starving in the Bronx
too.

CASH RULES EVERYTHING AROUND ME[46]

numbers run on the side of a building
somewhere in
New York City
a constant going
ever-moving
number.
tallying
the amount
of
debt
we owe
other countries

---

46 "C.R.E.A.M." is a classic tale by the rap group Wu-Tang Clan. Go listen.

THE COOL[47]

Hip Hop
is a distinct
art form
created by us
for us

started out of rebellion
from the mouths of Black and Brown
women and men
who look like me
like us

Hip Hop raised me
to carve stories
and sprinkle them with
Black joy
with Black hope
with Blackness
with us

it toughened my edges
showed me
the beauty in struggle
the beauty in beats
it was both this,
and that
and all the in-between.
the beauty of us
is the cool

---

47 This is a spoken word piece. Read it out loud. See how it feels on your tongue.
Swallow it and repeat.

hypocrisy inside, hypocrisy outside

THE TALK #23

when my uncle and aunt
came out
and
welcomed
Shirley
in
the brownstone in Brooklyn
which was usually filled with
noise.
laughter.
chatter.
and love
was quiet

very
very
Quiet.

THE BINARY

today lawmakers voted
to take
away
another thing
withdraw
another comfort
stop
progress to:
        queer rights
        human rights
        voting rights
        your rights
        our rights

they've perfected ways to get us to hate,
one another
live and lie
pit brother against sister
        silent cries

tomorrow you will
        cast a vote
        White or Black
        North or South
        Him or Her
        Right or wrong
        to "protect"
        to control
        to shield
binary boxes
for a binary world

MISOGYNOIR (NOUN/VERB)

/jen-ə-ˈrā-ʃ(ə-)n-əl/ /kərs/

:the dislike/contempt/ingrained prejudice for/against Black
women/girls

Much of what I know about masculinity I learned via Hip Hop.
I fell in love with Hip Hop easily. I'm not sure if it was the
storytelling, the rhythm or how bold it made me feel, but I lived
and breathed it.

Inside. Hip Hop is a part of our culture. Black culture. African
American culture. Storytelling, over beats made by us for us. And
I loved everything about it except for one thing. I hated how Hip
Hop treated femmes/girls/women.

It was no question that at its inception, Hip Hop was a male-
dominated industry. And the women who were allowed to be a
part were far and few between. Like it didn't want to make space
for us. Like it held a grudge against Black women.

It wasn't gentle to us. Didn't allow us to simply be. I didn't like
how it shoved Missy in a box. Didn't like how it pitted Foxy
against Lil' Kim.[48] Like there was only *one way* to be a Black Hip
Hop girlie, and that one way was defined by and for men.

But I loved the culture, so I was conflicted.

---

48 As if there isn't room for both.

BLACK FEMINISM AND RESPECTABILITY POLITICS

I learned just as much from Lil' Kim as I did bell hooks
about love
and forgiveness
about being a Black woman

I learned just as much from Queen Latifah as I have Toni
Morrison
about strength
and storytelling
about being a Black woman

I learned just as much from Megan Thee Stallion as I did Alice
Walker
about perseverance
and preservation
about being a Black woman

I've learned that boxes
can
not
contain
us

THE WAR ON WOKE[49]

is really about
accountability right?
What else could it be?

---

49 This is a 5-7-5 haiku.

HOOD (NOUN/VERB)
/hŭd/
:an under-resourced inner-city community inhabited by low
income and/or marginalized groups

Once I started leaving my neighborhood, I became more aware
of other boxes. Specifically about how the world perceives Black
girls from the hood. At school. On the train. In my new job. It
didn't matter where. In these new spaces, I felt like I was under a
microscope.

The way we talk. The way we walk. The things we say, and
sometimes the things we don't.

The world saw the hood as one dimensional. A place to pillage,
but never to acknowledge (or credit). A place to imitate, but never
to compensate. At this time, Hip Hop was taking center stage
in America, so everyone wanted to be down. Down with Black
culture. Down with Hip Hop culture.

Inside. In school, I watched white students equate Black culture
with hood culture and try us on like chic outfits. They butchered
the language, and bastardized the fashion. Black-faced our
mannerisms and profited off our swag . . . until the allure wore off.

Outside. I watched Pop culture equate Black culture with
hood culture and try us on like chic outfits. They butchered
the language, and bastardized the fashion. Black-faced our
mannerisms and profited off our swag . . . until the allure wore
off.[50]

---

50 Or it was no longer profitable.

Everybody wanna be Black until it's time to be Black

AAVE[51]

it is our language
we don't need you to like it
and it's not for sale

---

51 This is a 5-7-5 haiku.

THE QUEEN AND I

(For Dana Elaine Owens)

I fell in love with lyric
because she
weaved ghetto stories
into Pop hits
full stop.

painted our stories
in beautiful brown hues
on television and in film
full stop.

she
made strength out of struggle
and not in that
poverty porn
type of way
in that
40-Year-Old Version[52]
dope
Black
girl
type
of
way
full stop.

---

52 MUST WATCH: *The 40-Year-Old Version*

POVERTY PORN (PROPER NOUN)

/ˈpä-vər-tē pôrn/
:the exploitation of the living conditions of the poor/
impoverished, and/or under-resourced communities

Not going to college wasn't an option for me. Ma made that very clear during my senior year. She didn't care that I had just gotten a raise at the after-school program I was working at. She didn't care that I was taking driving lessons and was saving to buy a car. And she definitely didn't care that I had a new boyfriend, who, according to her, was the reason I had been "smelling myself" lately.

My sister was gone, and I was going to college. End of discussion.

When it was time to write my college essay, the counselor told me that I had a very interesting *story*. Telling it, in addition to my grades, would help me get into college and get a scholarship to pay for it. Because no one in my family had ever gone to college, she helped me write essays, complete applications, file for financial aid, and organize college tours. So when it came time to craft the college essay, I followed her lead as well. I remember her pushing me to talk about my upbringing. She told me to *dig deep* and talk about being from the ghetto. She said talking about how hard my life was would solidify my spot.

In my initial draft, I wrote about being from the Bronx. I wrote about being a part of a diverse community. A hybrid mix of African American, Caribbean, and Latin American cultures. I wrote about how these three worlds collided in the Bronx and Brooklyn—overlapping traditions, customs, and music. I wrote about how my ancestors had created something out of nothing— legends out of oral tradition, music out of pain, and comfort food out of scraps.

She did not see the beauty in this story. She wanted the college admissions counselors to feel sympathy for me. She wanted me to talk about my mother's drug addiction or talk about gang violence in our neighborhood. There is only one narrative in these types of stories. Yes, my mother was once a young girl who made some bad decisions. But behind the story was the story of her going to rehab and enrolling in college courses. The counselor didn't want that story though.

She wanted me to write it again.

So I rewrote it. End of discussion.

BLACK WOMEN FROM THE HOOD DON'T GROW UP TO BE WRITERS

before I left for college my counselor told me to "be practical"
but what I heard was
Black women from the hood don't grow up to be writers

she reminded me,
often.
that I was First Generation
      college student
      (then hopefully) college graduate
      (then hopefully) graduate student

which meant,
I was carrying the torch for my
      younger brother
      younger cousins
      (then hopefully) unborn children
      (then hopefully) their unborn children
      and all the unborn Black and Brown children for
generations and generations to come

and because I was smart,
she said,
I would get a scholarship
would be sought after,
requested.
favored.
and being from the hood,
well . . .
was just a bonus!
but what I heard was
P.W.I.s and big universities love poverty porn!

she ended with
any school would be lucky to have me
only
Black women from the hood don't grow up to be writers

P.W.I. (PROPER NOUN)

/pē/ˈdə-bəl yü/ eye
:predominantly white institution

When it was time to start thinking about college, I applied to schools all across America. Some of them were P.W.I.s, and some were Historically Black Colleges and Universities (HBCU). In my heart, I wanted my college experience to mirror the one from *A Different World.*[53] Wanted to be around melanated folk who understood me. Understood my culture and my background. I think I must have applied to over twenty colleges.

And then the acceptance letters started to roll in. I'm not sure if it was the cringe essay or my grades . . . but I got into all of them. Like, every single one.

After all of the acceptance letters came in, however, Ma and I sat down to look at the cost of tuition and room and board. I knew she didn't have the funds to pay for college, and I knew my dad didn't have it either.[54] After tallying up how much it would cost. Room. Board. Books. Tuition. My final decision came down to financing.

I knew that I didn't want to be in debt after college[55] and even though I was awarded financial aid, it wouldn't cover all of the fees (or food). And I couldn't stomach adding another thing to my mother's plate.

---

53 The television show *A Different World* was a huge part of my unboxing.
54 My anxiety was at an all-time high that year.
55 Predatory student-loan practices have been and continue to be a huge (and heavy) barrier for Black students after high school.

EMANCIPATION[56]

On January 1, 1863, they were freed
no longer belonging
to.
of.
for.

Jubilee could be heard; the New Year marked a new term
No longer obliged to
be.
stay.
sit.

and as the dust settled, the clarity of freedom loomed . . .
marks no longer exclamation as questions gathered . . .
what?
when?
where?

And like Bluebeard's wife —
Revealing . . . but at *what* cost?
No longer needing to dream and pray for

Freedom,
Freedom
Freedom.

---

56 RESEARCH: Juneteenth

MIGRATION

For the souls' progression they walked   they walked
from the South—clay roads   from the South
past calling Gallows   past
through brooks that were once home   that
with the taste of freedom at their fingertips. taste
Ignorance holds no hope here   ignorance.
Looking to a new day they walk   to

For the souls' satisfaction they trudged   satisfaction.
through back alleys and the back-bus-seats   Through
ignoring the Jim Crows that follow the procession Jim Crow,
and a Lynch letter is still in play.   and Lynch.
waiting for falter.   waiting
waiting to break them.   waiting
Looking to a new day they walk   to a new day.

For the souls' rejoice   souls rejoice
to the North in the face of temptation   to the North.
they carried Jazz to brownstone streets   They carried
littered blocks with happiness   happiness.
Quenched thirst with demands.   Quenched thirst.
And filled stomachs   And filled stomachs
with hope   with hope.

I USED TO LOVE H.I.M.

I met him on the corner of blues and jazz[57]
I let him read my poetry while he spit his scat
on Loves' migration[58] we floated upward
on a Porter car to Chicago
past Dixie lines[59] and gallow'd trees
we held hands like our breath depended on it,
to city-scapes where everything mirrored vibrant portraits
Lawrence-lilacs, Bearden-blues, Parks-purples and Douglas-denims
told our unborn children of journeys through the night
to freedom.
(And the food was just right.)

I met him on the corner of blues and jazz,
I let him read my poetry while he spit his scat,
on loves' migration we floated upward
on a Porter car to Harlem.
on a groove we corrected dreams deferred[60]
and band-aided them from running
loved on brownstone building tops
below neighborhood rent parties,[61] where
Billie[62] bellowed, and The Duke[63] dragged Bessie's[64] bass over
Morton's[65] melodies
to freedom.
(And the music was just right.)

57 An American music form created by African Americans musicians in the 1920s
58 From 1910–1970, newly freed enslaved people migrated to Northern cities to
get away from oppressive conditions of the South.
59 The Mason–Dixon line was the border separating the North from the South.
Many African Americans crossed it during the Great Migration.
60 "Harlem" (also known as "A Dream Deferred") was written by Langston
Hughes; go read it!
61 RESEARCH: Rent parties
62 Billie Holiday was an African American jazz and blues singer.
63 Duke Ellington was an African American jazz and swing artist and composer.
64 Bessie Smith was an African American blues singer famous during the
Harlem Renaissance.
65 Jelly Roll Morton was an African American jazz pianist and composer.

I met him on the corner of blues and jazz,
I let him read my poetry while he spit his scat,
my renaissance[66] started with him
on a Porter car to hope
in the hue of a sunset
in the backdrop of the city
in the wake of the South
the North had set us free.

---

66 The Harlem Renaissance was a magical time for African Americans in New York City, one that spurred art, music, and visual media that we consume to this day.

AND THE ONES WE SHED

III – AND THE ONES WE SHED

What if we could just be?

THE BOXES WE SHED

are our elders' wildest dreams
it's Mary's *Real Love*
wrapped in a custom
Dapper Dan suit
it's a one of a kind
—ever growing
—ever learning
—ever healing
shape shifting
type of love
that allows
—and listens.
it's
a stick-to-your-ribs
space of your choosing
a destiny
designed by you
—a
Becoming[67]
masterpiece.

---

67 MUST READ: Michelle Obama's *Becoming*

be gentle on yourself

FOR BLACK GIRLS III[68]

design your own path
build your own community
live authentically

---

68 This is a 5-7-5 haiku.

WHITE PEOPLE SHIT (NOUN)

/(h)wīt/ /ˈpēpəl/ /ʃit/

:typically associated with activities of leisure, extreme sports, and
anything that steps too far outside of Black culture norms

I was a full emo teenager by the end of high school. Call it the
hormones or . . . life, but I hated everything and everyone. My
siblings. My mother. My neighborhood. My job. I retreated into
my journal and books. My poetry was dark and moody, and the
music I listened to was a blend of anything angsty and uber
dramatic moody songs. My music taste went from strictly Hip Hop
and R&B to alternative rock-and-roll.

Music choice, I would soon learn, was another one of those things
that some people used to define Blackness.

Inside. My mother had vinyl records all over the house. Records
from her time abroad and ones that she collected in the states. A
few of her cousins were in rap groups, so music was a big part of
her life. She did not limit herself to specific genres. She was heavy
into disco, funk, and had tons of reggae albums. On Sundays there
was always a record on rotation, and cleaning supplies in the air.

Outside. Black girls got to listen to Hip Hop and R&B. Only.
Full stop. When I started playing Alanis Morissette and Fefe
Dobson on rotations, people looked at me like I had three eyes.
Not because these artists were white (because Fefe is definitely
a sister) but because this, along with many other random things,
was deemed White People Shit. As if Black girls from the hood
could only listen to specific things.

As if.[69]

---

69 *I will not have my life narrowed down. I will not bow down to somebody else's
whim or to someone else's ignorance.* —bell hooks

KEEP IT UNDER CONTROL

I suffered from anxiety
in silence.
learned to keep it
under control.
code-switched coping into
mannequin smiles   *always with a smile.*
learned to swallow the lumps
that gathered in my throat.
dabbed away the sweat
pooled under my arms.
mastered techniques
       to mask
       to hide
boxed it up,
tucked it away and
took it to college with me.

THE TALK #31

before I left for college Ma
sat me down
to discuss
drugs
and drinking

said that I needed to keep my wits
about me
know who my
true friends were

and most importantly
trust
my
instincts

WHY ARE ALL THE BLACK KIDS SITTING TOGETHER IN THE CAFETERIA[70]

I wouldn't have made it through college
without community
without
Black Student Union
without my sisters

---

70 BOOK RECOMMENDATION: *Why Are All the Black Kids Sitting Together in the Cafeteria* by Beverly Daniel Tatum

BLACK GIRL NOD

There is this unspoken thing
we do
as black women
it's a small gesture
so small you could miss it
      and if you haven't been raised in the culture you are sure
to
a nod
so subtle
so small
it says:
      i see you
      i am with you
      and if shit goes down
i got your back.

FORDHAM[71]

In college
bad habits turn into
things we do, with a side of shrug
balancing two hours of sleep
and fourteen-credit course loads
becomes a skill, and
Thursdays
       shimmy in the weekend

in the café
brown cups of irregularities
replace breakfast and dinner.
Hiroshima clouds milk in
just the right amount of liquid disturbance

it is here
over cracked cups of the past
that I meet you

we danced through the city's neighborhoods
meatballs in Little Italy
beef patties in Brooklyn
poetry at the Nuyorican
and graffiti in the Bronx
two naïve natives
donning burgundy and gray

at graduation we gushed
promising stars we could never touch
I still remember the way you take your coffee.

---

71 Published in ZZyZx WriterZ *Intersections* Anthology Reading, 2017

MASKING (VERB)

/'mask-ŋ/

:the act of hiding or suppressing symptoms of a mental health condition

I struggled in college. In addition to my anxiety, I had a hard time academically. In high school I'd graduated at the top of my class, but I was drowning in college. There was so much that I hadn't learned. Words and worlds that I did not know.

Outside. I felt inadequate compared to my classmates. I didn't have money for anything outside the meal plan/cafeteria. Couldn't afford college books, and in between class and working, I didn't have much spare time. To the outside world, I'm sure they saw a hardworking studious Black girl who spent most of her free time in the library.

That first semester of college, every paper I wrote received a mediocre grade (at best) and I was recommended to the writing center. I felt like my professors were speaking in a different language and I felt my mask starting to slip.

Inside. All I wanted to do was scream.

be gentle with yourself

THERAPY[72]

The invisible	The invisible
line drawn in sand.	line
WE don't go to therapy.	we don't
talk about family outside?	talk about
Black folks don't do that	don't
We address it behind closed doors	address,
keep things in the closet	keep
but maybe . . . when it's just US	us
WE can admit, being in	in
the hamster wheel	the hamster wheel
is exhausting	*it's* exhausting

---

72 If you are seeking therapy resources, consider Therapyforblackgirls.com and Therapyforblackmen.org.

THE TALK #29

I started going to therapy
        freshman year
I learned, that
when I needed a break
I should take
a
damn
break

which was really   *i mean really*
really hard

I'd gone my entire life thinking
stay strong
push through
you can take on more   *but Black girls are not superheroes*
and so I did

and then
I cracked
and everything
came tumbling down

THE MISEDUCATION OF ANGELA SHANTÉ

I almost quit college
freshman year
overwhelmed with
trying
learning
back-learning
re-learning
un-learning

round and round
we go

I hadn't read most of the books
didn't get any of the references
a never-ending game of catch up

round and round
we go

GET OFF THE HAMSTER WHEEL[73]
(dedicated to the Nap Ministry)

don't want to hustle
don't want to work 'til I die
I want to live life.

---

73 This is a 5-7-5 haiku.

CHASING RAINBOWS

there's a guilt attached to Black self-care
tied to Black rest
and
Black joy

myths hemmed
into the fabric
of our chromosomes

tall tales sprinkled
into the drinking water
of our country

but I've written enough poems
about dead Black babies
to know that they still dream about rainbows,
even on the other side.

THE WOMEN I'VE LOVED

have been,
brown
and sweet
      wide smiles
      on summer nights

taught me,
how to be soft
and strong
      how to laugh
      with my eyes
      and cry from
      my gut

these women,
Brown-faced
like me
Are my safe space
in a world
      hard on Black babies
      hard on Black bodies
      hard on Black beauty
      hard on Black birth
      hard on Black girls.

REST

isn't a word we associated
with
Blackness

from childhood
we are taught to
work.
          mother
take care of,
one another.

how hard it is for us to see
her as
anything
more than
a worker
a savior
a mother
healer
daughter
wife.

What if we could just be free?

BECOMING[74]

never stop growing
becoming a masterpiece
takes time sis, *real* time.

---

74 This is a 5-7-5 haiku.

WHO AM I?[75]

I am you,
for you are me
I stand on the feet of those who've come before me
breaking down doors to warn me
> the minds of the lost fall to trickery
> *and you shall wear your helmet today . . .*

I am you, for you are me
I ride on the backs of my people who have
made history
those who have chosen to speak
in order to guide me
> sat so I can stand free
> *and our hands are not shackled anymore . . .*

I am the dream that Martin left,
the spirit that made Harriet flee
through the trees that swing the gallows' pleas

I am the gumption that X had when he began to read
and see,
and believe
> *there is always more to learn and always space to grow.*

they paved the way for you and me
to be.
who
we want
to be.

I am my ancestors' wildest dreams.

---

75 This is a spoken word piece. It is meant to be read out loud. See how it feels
on your tongue. Swallow it and repeat.

HOME[76]

(for Nikki Giovanni)

I remember . . . there was once a time . . . I wanted to be you . . .
wanted to Afro-out my life . . . color my brown face . . . black . . .
red . . . green . . . I thought it would make you happy . . . this rebel
child . . . who taught . . . apartheid . . . Rap Brown . . . who stopped
processing her hair . . . because I knew it had . . . institutionalized
my mind . . . my appearance . . . changed my spirit . . . to the
always wanting-to-be . . . instead of the . . . I am . . . thought it
would show dedication . . . prove to you . . . to myself . . . that I was
. . . a writer . . . and a feminist . . . an educator . . . a revolutionary
. . . not only on the weekends . . . that I was living outside of . . .
and . . . beyond the boxes that others tried to put me in . . . you in
. . . her in . . . them in . . . but I remembered . . . that being me . . .
meant that I was you . . . coming from Knoxville and The Bronx.
. . being both 28 and 68 . . . knowing too much . . . and having
digested too little . . . brown locks with speckles of . . . gray . . . and
journeys . . . and hope . . . I began to remember . . . to understand
. . . to write . . . and rewrite . . . not of only burning . . . pink . . .
ribbons . . . frills . . . and the flag . . . but how to imprint myself
. . . on someone . . . as you have . . . left a tattoo . . . of love . . . of
knowing . . . on me . . . and I realized that . . . without this thing
. . . of stage . . . of voice . . . of tradition . . . I had no voice . . . could
be silenced . . . could be cast . . . only Black . . . only female . . . only
able to ribbon my poems with kisses . . . instead I know. . . and
dream . . . and have awakened dreams . . . they speak through me
. . . from voices of women before . . . and women to come . . . so I
make my contribution . . . I take up my pen . . . and I write.

---

76 A spoken word piece previously published in *KGB Bar* Literary Magazine

What if we could just be?[77]

77 *For me, becoming isn't about arriving somewhere or achieving*
a certain aim. I see it instead as forward motion, a means of
evolving, a way to reach continuously toward a better self.
The journey doesn't end.
—Michelle Obama, *Becoming*

READERS GUIDE

DISCUSSION QUESTIONS

1. Not every "talk" an adult has a good lesson/moral in *The Unboxing of a Black Girl*. Which of the "The Talk" poem(s) did you find problematic? Why? Which of the "The Talk" poem(s) did you find helpful? Why? Which of these lessons/talks do you think are important for teens to learn? Why?

2. For one section title, Angela writes, "Black girls learn duality early. Too early." What does duality mean? Many of the vignettes/stories in *The Unboxing of a Black Girl* switch between inside/outside commentary. How does this change your understanding of duality? What "boxes" are discussed in these pieces? How are they similar? Conflicting?

3. Angela uses the movie *The Wiz* as a metaphor to discuss personal and political topics/boxes. What connections can you make between the movie/characters and the pieces in *The Unboxing of a Black Girl*?

4. For one section title, Angela writes, "When do Black girls lose their childhood?" When does a person become an adult? What are positive and negative reasons one might not feel like a child anymore?

5. For one section title, Angela writes, "Everybody wanna be Black until it's time to be Black." What does this phrase mean to you? What aspects of Black culture have been co-opted by the mainstream? What fashions, words, and art forms originated with Black creators/culture?

6. In *The Unboxing of a Black Girl*, Angela quotes Dr. Martin Luther King Jr., saying, "Sometimes to move forward, we have to go backward." Do you think the past influences the present? What historical moments does Angela reference, and how do you think they are impacting the world today?

7. Angela talks about self-care in the section "And the Ones We Shed." What instances of self-care did you notice in *The Unboxing of a Black Girl?* Why does Angela discuss the importance of rest and being gentle with/on yourself?

8. "For me, becoming isn't about arriving somewhere or achieving a certain aim. I see it instead as forward motion, a means of evolving, a way to reach continuously toward a better self. The journey doesn't end."
    —Michelle Obama, *Becoming*

    This quote about how people are always changing and growing ends the book. What do you think are some of the biggest lessons Angela learned in her childhood/ unboxing? What lessons have you learned from this book? What are you inspired to become?

REFERENCES AND RESEARCH

Music Referenced in This Book

- "Public Service Announcement," Jay-Z
- "It's Not Right but It's Okay," written by LaShawn Daniels, Rodney Jerkins, Fred Jerkins III, Isaac Phillips, Toni Estes; recorded by the one and only Whitney Houston
- "Juicy," The Notorious B.I.G
- "Strange Fruit," recorded by Nina Simone
- "American Terrorist," Lupe Fiasco
- "The Miseducation of Lauryn Hill," Lauryn Hill
- "Just Another Day. . . ," recorded by Queen Latifah
- "C.R.E.A.M." Wu-Tang Clan

TV/Film/Stage Referenced in This Book

- *Fences*, August Wilson (play)
- *Get Out*, Jordan Peele (film)
- *The Wiz*, Quincy Jones (film)
- *The Color Purple*, Alice Walker (play)
- *Living Single*, Queen Latifah (show)
- *A Different World*, Bill Cosby and Debbie Allen (show)
- *Love Jones*, Theodore Witcher (film)
- *The 40-Year-Old Version*, Radha Blank (film)

Literature Referenced in This Book

- *All About Love*, bell hooks
- *Talking Back*, bell hooks
- *Teaching to Transgress*, bell hooks
- *The Meaning of Freedom*, Angela Davis
- *Women, Race & Class*, Angela Davis
- *Love Poems*, Nikki Giovanni
- *I Am Loved*, Nikki Giovanni
- *The Sun Is So Quiet*, Nikki Giovanni
- *A Library*, Nikki Giovanni

- *Rosa*, Nikki Giovanni
- *Shake Loose My Skin*, Sonia Sanchez
- *The Bluest Eye*, Toni Morrison
- "The Breast Giver", Mahasweta Devi
- *The Autobiography of Malcolm X*, Alex Haley and Malcolm X
- *Becoming*, Michelle Obama
- *Rest Is Resistance: A Manifesto*, Tricia Hersey
- *I Know Why the Caged Bird Sings*, Maya Angelou
- *Patriarchy Blues*, Frederick Joseph
- *The Color Purple*, Alice Walker
- *Montage of a Dream Deferred*, Langston Hughes
- *Women Who Run With the Wolves: Myths and Stories of the Wild Woman Archetype*, Clarissa Pinkola Estés
- *Push*, Sapphire
- *for colored girls who have considered suicide / when the rainbow is enuf*, Ntozake Shange

Topics Referenced in This Book

- Gender roles
- The adultification of Black girls
- Brown paper bag test
- Food deserts
- Strong Black woman trope
- Intergenerational trauma
- Intergenerational healing
- Segregated schools in the 1970s
- Napping and rest as resistance
- Gentle parenting
- Sexual assault

Unboxing Topics to Research

- How to play Spades
- Redlining
- School desegregation in America
- Code-switching
- Medical racism
- The history of policing in America
- Roe vs. Wade
- Capitalism
- Misogyny/Misogynoir
- Emancipation
- The Great Migration
- The Harlem Renaissance
- Jazz
- The Mason–Dixon Line

INSPIRATION

TV Programs That Helped with My Unboxing

- *Living Single*
- *A Different World*
- *Girlfriends*
- *Moesha*
- *The Parkers*
- *Sister, Sister*

Literary Elders Who Helped with My Unboxing

- bell hooks
- Maya Angelou
- Alice Walker
- Toni Morrison
- Angela Davis
- Nikki Giovanni
- Octavia Butler
- Sonia Sanchez
- Phillis Wheatly
- Jacqueline Woodson
- Ntozake Shange

Artists Who Helped with My Unboxing

- Nina Simone
- Salt-N-Pepa
- Erykah Badu
- Jill Scott
- Lauryn Hill
- Queen Latifah
- TLC
- Lisa "Left Eye" Lopes
- Lil' Kim
- Foxy Brown
- Jacob Lawrence
- Romare Bearden
- Aaron Douglas
- Billie Holiday
- Duke Ellington
- Bessie Smith
- Jelly Roll Morton
- Janelle Monáe
- Prince
- Megan Thee Stallion

RESOURCES

- Therapyforblackgirls.com
- Therapyforblackmen.org
- rainn.org

Unboxing Music Playlist (Curated by Angela Shanté)

- "INTRO," India Shawn with Kaye Fox
- "Holding Space," Mayyadda
- "Basquiat," Jamila Woods and Saba
- "Ten Toes Down," Talibah Safiya
- "Weary," Solange
- "Unconventional Ways," Jazzyfatnastees
- "Shine," Cleo Sol
- "Up and Down," Talibah Safiya
- "Wire," Ama Lou
- "Rose in the Dark," Cleo Sol
- "Cranes in the Sky," Solange
- "Sweet Blue," Cleo Sol
- "Dreams," Cosima
- "Mountains," Charlotte Day Wilson
- "Her Light," Cleo Sol
- "girlfriend," Hemlocke Springs
- "R.I.P. Captain Save-a-Heaux," Mayyadda
- "Special," Lizzo featuring SZA
- "Enough for Love," Kelela
- "Get Free," Mereba
- "Crazy, Classic, Life," Janelle Monáe

ACKNOWLEDGMENTS

I'm eternally grateful for my editor, Tamara Grasty. I knew from our initial conversation that my words would be safe with you. Thank you for guiding me in completing this (and for making me dig deeper). Also, thank you for the entire team at Page Street YA who contributed to this collection (especially the creative team!). I couldn't imagine this project being in anyone else's hands.

During the making of this project, my grandmother and aunt became ancestors, and . . . well . . . I'm still processing. I'm sad that they will not get the chance to see this project come to fruition, but comforted in the time spent with them while finalizing this book. I'm grateful for the interviews, late night phone calls, and cross-country road trip we had right before they transitioned . . . .

And most importantly, I'm happy I was able to document this healing process with them.

ABOUT THE AUTHOR

Angela Shanté is a former K–12 classroom teacher who started her writing career as a poet/spoken word artist. Angela received her Master of Fine Arts from the City College of New York, where she grew up. These days, the native New Yorker isn't sticking to one coast/industry (or box) and divides her time as an educator and creative in Los Angeles and her home borough of the Boogie Down Bronx.